COACH YOURSELF BETTER, FAST

DO CHANGE BETTER

Based on *How to be a Change Superhero*
by Lucinda Carney

First published in Great Britain by Practical Inspiration Publishing, 2024

© Lucinda Carney and Practical Inspiration Publishing, 2024

The moral rights of the author have been asserted

ISBN 9781788606738   (paperback)
      9781788606752   (epub)
      9781788606745   (Kindle)

All rights reserved. This book, or any portion thereof, may not be reproduced without the express written permission of the publisher.

Every effort has been made to trace copyright holders and to obtain their permission for the use of copyright material. The publisher apologizes for any errors or omissions and would be grateful if notified of any corrections that should be incorporated in future reprints or editions of this book.

Want to bulk-buy copies of this book for your team and colleagues? We can customize the content and co-brand *Do Change Better* to suit your business's needs.

Please email info@practicalinspiration.com for more details.

Practical Inspiration Publishing

Contents

Series introduction iv

Introduction 1

Day 1: Courage 4

Day 2: Connecting with strategy 14

Day 3: Corroboration 25

Day 4: Communication and collaboration 33

Day 5: Change and personality 50

Day 6: Cultures, values and leadership 65

Day 7: Build your change league 81

Day 8: Planning large-scale change 94

Day 9: Build your communication plan 104

Day 10: The process of large-scale change 116

Conclusion 126

Endnotes 128

Series introduction

Welcome to *6-Minute Smarts*!

This is a series of very short books with one simple purpose: to introduce you to ideas that can make life and work better, and to give you time and space to think about how those ideas might apply to *your* life and work.

Each book introduces you to ten powerful ideas, but ideas on their own are useless – that's why each idea is followed by self-coaching questions to help you work out the 'so what?' for you in just six minutes of exploratory writing. Because that's where the magic happens.

Whatever you're facing, there's a *6-Minute Smarts* book just for you. And once you've learned how to coach yourself through a new idea, you'll be smarter for life.

Find out more...

Introduction

Change has become the new normal at work, but many changes are still poorly planned, communicated or implemented. Most managers and employees haven't been trained in how to deliver or react to change. Even people with transformation or change in their job title are often poorly prepared for the complex requirements of managing change well. Ultimately, poorly managed change results in reduced business outcomes and can leave people emotionally damaged by the experience. So, isn't it time to 'do change' better?

This book is for anyone who wants to feel better equipped to manage, deliver or respond to change in the workplace. We'll explore the skills and traits that can be helpful when involved in change and consider how we can develop these. We'll also consider the human and cultural responses to change that can make it feel smooth or bumpy. Finally, we'll explore how to bring this all together into a change 'Master Plan' that will allow you to utilize the strengths of a team and understand clearly how to plan and deliver large-scale change successfully.

This book is primarily aimed at those involved in organizational or business change. That said, several chapters will also be relevant if you're experiencing personal change too. Ultimately, this book will be relevant to anyone involved in designing or implementing organizational change, which is most of us nowadays. We'll use the term Change Agent in this context; someone committed to 'Doing Change Better' in their organization by taking people with them and achieving the desired goals of the change.

I hope that you'll find this book easy to read yet highly applicable and practical, whatever your level of experience. I've tried to strike a balance between theory, personal examples and practical tools that you can pick up and run with.

- Chapters 1 to 4 look at the individual skills that we need to develop for us to become effective 'Change Agents'.
- Chapters 5 and 6 focus on 'Change Challenges', including people who resist and challenge change, making your life harder, as

Introduction

well as specific hurdles that we come across during change, which are often cultural or structural.
- Chapters 7 to 10 help you to build a 'Change Master Plan', working with others to deliver large-scale change successfully.

You can read it all through in one go, or you can treat it as a day-by-day mini-course. It's entirely up to you.

Let's go!

Day 1

Courage

Courage is the foundation of any successful Change Agent's skillset. Delivering change is rarely easy – we need to know when to speak and when to listen. Often opposition comes from the most senior people in the organization, so it takes courage to politely challenge that resistance. We need to get to know and master our own emotions and behaviours, and learn how to engage in persuasion, communication and collaboration.

Challenging resistance from senior colleagues

To be an effective Change Agent we need to have the courage to talk to people on a personal level, whatever their level of seniority. They're human too (easy to forget, sometimes) and they'll also have natural responses to any change. A courageous Change Agent needs to tackle this head on, particularly with key sponsors or other highly visible or influential individuals. Try making personal contact at an early stage to explain the change, agreeing the key messages and gaining explicit commitment. Once you have that, it makes it easier to politely remind them of this if they go on to behave differently.

Effective Change Agents need to wear multiple hats without 'faking it'. As we improve our self-awareness we have more choices about how we behave. If we want to deliver change successfully, we need to be flexible enough to both lead and follow. To be diplomatic and challenging, or open yet restrained, this requires high levels of self-awareness and self-control, otherwise known as emotional intelligence.

Emotional intelligence (EI)

American psychologist Daniel Goleman identified five different aspects of EI: self-awareness, self-control, self-motivation, empathy and social skills.

Self-awareness

This is our own understanding of 'what makes us tick': what motivates us, our personality and the way we typically react to situations or how we come across to others.

For example, I tend to talk quickly, which gives the impression that I'm nervous or excited, even when I'm not. Appearing nervous or excited is often inappropriate at work, so I can use this self-awareness and choose to speak more slowly.

Self-control (or self-regulation)

Self-control is something that can be learned; it's a bit like a muscle that can benefit from exercise. Understanding that certain behaviours tend to result in negative outcomes may motivate us to exercise more self-control. Or we may exercise self-control on demand by considering what we want as an outcome. You were probably told as a child to 'count to ten' before responding when angry. It's still good advice. We can use those ten seconds to consider a range of possible responses and the likely outcome of each, then select the best response for the situation. The best response is rarely our automatic response, so this usually involves self-control, but it does generate better long-term relationships and results.

Self-motivation

High levels of EI usually indicate high levels of self-motivation, the ability to determine what needs to be done and to do it without outside influence. Self-motivated people find the need and determination to complete tasks, even under challenging circumstances, without either giving up or needing external encouragement.

Those with high levels of self-motivation and drive are going to be better at seeing any change through to completion, including overcoming the many obstacles and setbacks that may be encountered along the way. The best way to develop self-motivation is by creating a clear vision then setting and keeping small commitments that align with it.

Empathy

When we demonstrate that we understand the emotions of others, we're showing empathy. Empathy can be evidenced non-verbally, through body language and facial expressions, or verbally, with phrases such as 'I understand' or 'that sounds frustrating'. Empathy is particularly important for people during change. There are four main stages of what's known as the transition or change curve: denial, resistance, exploration and commitment. If people get stuck in denial or resistance because they don't feel that their concerns are being heard or addressed satisfactorily, then the entire project may fail.

Social skills

Having good social skills means being able to interact positively and build relationships with others. It's really a culmination of the four other aspects of EI, with a healthy dose of communication skills thrown in. Essentially, EI starts with being able to understand our own emotions (self-awareness), then learning to manage them (self-control) and using them to set and achieve goals (self-motivation). Once we can understand and manage ourselves then we can start to understand the emotions and feelings of others (empathy) and finally choose the best communication style and behaviours to influence them or to work together positively (social skills).

Transformational leadership

EI takes us on the journey from leading ourselves to leading others, and someone who is effective at leading others through change can be described as a 'transformational leader'.

Courage

Transformational leadership as a concept was introduced by leadership expert and presidential biographer James MacGregor Burns (2003)[1] and further developed by researcher Bernard M. Bass (2005).[2] Essentially, it's all about those in leadership positions providing the personal touch and building trust, which in turn inspires others to follow.

None of this is about pretending to 'be' something to manipulate others to change. We might get away with that once, but not in the long run. Effective Change Agents start by leading themselves, by developing their personal EI and behaving consistently in line with their values and doing what they say they will. This consistency builds trust, which makes people choose to follow them.

Transformational leadership skills are important when leading change – particularly culture change, which demands the empowerment, engagement and motivation of individuals. The common alternative – transactional leadership – is more about working within the status quo, focusing on management activities such as compliance, productivity, structure or hierarchy – in other words, 'doing' change, rather than leading it.

It's important to demonstrate transformational leadership skills when dealing with the human aspects of change, and transactional leadership skills when we manage the systems and processes involved in embedding change; both are essential if we want to achieve long-lasting results.

Sometimes, however, it's just as important to have the courage to follow others as it is to lead.

Having the courage to follow

The TED Talk by Derek Sivers called 'How to start a movement' (2010) shows a video of a man dancing alone in a field at a music festival. He's waving his arms around and dancing crazily, being watched with curiosity by many other seated festival-goers. He's clearly enjoying himself and doesn't seem the least bit self-conscious. After a while, a second person joins him – 'The First Follower', as Sivers puts it. This First Follower emulates the crazy, unselfconscious dance moves – somehow giving the act credibility. Then a few more join in and before long there are more people up and dancing the crazy dance than there are sitting watching. Suddenly, it's cool to be part of the crazy dance movement.[3]

Change is all about creating a movement, and every movement needs a first, second and third follower. It takes as much courage to follow someone into the unknown, to back an early change and to give it credibility, as it does to start the change in

Courage

the first place. Effective Change Agents don't mind if they start a movement, or if they're simply the First Follower; delivering the change or creating the movement is their priority. It all starts with psychological courage – and it's up to us whether we choose to develop it or not.

✎ So what? Over to you...

1. What aspects of EI do you most need to develop?

2. What would it look like for you to demonstrate transformational rather than transactional leadership?

Courage

3. Where do you need to be more courageous when it comes to change at work?

Day 2
Connecting with strategy

A strategy defines the vision or plan of an organization; it's a concept, a design and an output. Change Agents help people understand how the proposed change connects to the overall strategy. If someone can see the connection between the change and an overall strategy or goal that they value, then they're more motivated to buy in to the change.

The Change Equation

Linking to strategy often requires us to tell a story, which may be about exciting positives or may also be about avoiding potential negatives. Richard Beckhard and Reuben Harris wrote about a formula for change known as the Change Equation in their book

Organizational Transitions: Managing Complex Change.[4] This change formula can be used as a structure around which to build our story:

C = [ABD] > X

Where C = making it happen, A = level of dissatisfaction with the status quo, B = desirability of the proposed change or end state, D = practicality of the change (knowledge of the next practical step, minimal risk and disruption) and X = cost of change. So, as Change Agents we're more likely to be able to deliver change if the multiplying effect of A, B and D is higher than the perceived cost of change to those affected. There are three key factors to consider here:

1. The rationale for change must be clearly laid out, linking to the strategy. This may be about explaining the current or future problems associated with the status quo, making the need to change seem inevitable.
2. The end goal or vision for the change needs to be communicated in an appealing way, focusing on the benefits of the change – both organizational and personal.
3. The initiative must appear to be well thought through and practical, reducing fear of the unknown and providing confidence that its achievement is possible.

Because the cost of change is always high in terms of uncertainty and upheaval, it's important to emphasize the benefits of the overall goal and link it to the strategy.

We all like to have a sense of purpose and find greater importance in what we're doing, perhaps to feel part of something bigger than ourselves. As Change Agents, if we want to influence people to behave in a certain way, we have to give them that sense of greater meaning.

Unfortunately, during change the communication focus is typically on *what* is going to change rather than *why* we're making the change, which often leads to resistance because people don't understand the bigger picture. Connecting with the strategy or vision encourages people to look up and to see the future first. The future might be positive and exciting with the change, or it might be negative and frightening without the change.

To build and communicate these powerful links with a positive or negative association, the Change Agent needs to ensure that the 'why', 'what' and 'how' of any change are understood at all levels of the organization. There can be multiple 'whys', 'whats' and 'hows' to ensure relevance and meaning to different audiences.

The quality and credibility of the strategy will be directly related to the effectiveness of the assumptions. Tools such as Porter and Tanner's (2003) PESTLE analysis below can be used to ensure that the rationale for any strategy change is well evidenced.[5]

Political factors

This may include likely government policies or changes, including tariffs, subsidies or immigration quotas, which can create perceived urgency; for example, many businesses relying on consultants in full-time positions moved to outsource staff when National Insurance costs went up.

Economic factors

National and global economic circumstances, whether we're in a recession or boom times, and exchange rates can all influence these factors; for example, we may choose to extend our house rather than move in order to avoid Stamp Duty.

Social factors

This is more about the trends within society, including demographic and cultural changes in expectations for products, services and working environments; for example, we may be motivated to move jobs because we have friends in a particular industry.

Technological factors

Clearly, this is a rapidly changing and potentially disruptive force that can create competitive advantage in terms of goods, services and access to both customers and workforce; for example, we may need to change processes to streamline testing or integrate artificial intelligence into customer support.

Legal factors

Legislation can provide compelling reasons to change in relation to governance; for example, the General Data Protection Regulation, or legislation that provides new market opportunities for products or solutions.

Environmental factors

This relates to changing attitudes on environmental practices. This can be bolstered by government legislation (legal) or incentives; for example, tax relief on green company cars (economic), which may make change more attractive.

A strategy enables organizations or businesses to survive and prosper. If the ability to achieve this purpose is threatened, then it creates the need to change. A restructure can offer a positive vision of a reskilled workforce that's able to beat the competition.

Let's look at how we reframe or reposition a message before we communicate it. You've probably heard the term 'golden thread' being referred to when setting objectives. This is the link between our goals or objectives and the overall business strategy that will help us understand why the change is necessary.

For example, a new company process requires all contractors to complete detailed timesheets with a breakdown of how much time was spent with which customer. By following the golden thread, we find that the actual purpose is to better allocate training costs to clients, to ensure that all training is billed accurately. The most important piece of information to be captured by the contractors is what they're spending the most time on; it's not about micro-accounting for time.

Strategies tend to be long-term, so however inspiring they are to begin with, they still require high levels of determination and resilience to see them through to fruition. This is why it's important to set key sub-goals or manageable milestones along the way in the confidence that they're taking us in the right direction over the longer term.

As Change Agents, we and others need to be able to clearly articulate answers to the following questions:

- Where are we now?
- Where do we need to go?
- Why do we need to go there?
- How will we get there (specifically)?

Most people are familiar with the concept of SMART goals – specific and stretching, measurable, achievable and agreed, relevant and time-bound. However, SMART really is far more than an acronym; it's well backed by behavioural science. One of the most effective ways of encouraging high performance is by agreeing clear goals and providing feedback against them (Locke & Latham, 1994).[6] Agreement is key to buy-in when setting goals and delivering change.

'Relevant' means ensuring the individual understands the relevance of the goal in relation to the strategy and potentially in relation to their own role or their own interests. If a goal is relevant to us, our buy-in will be greater.

Connecting with strategy

Any goal needs to be time-bound and this is especially important in large-scale change that goes on for months or even years. Having an overall target date or timescale to aim for is good. It provides a sense of progress, keeping people focused and on track.

Chan Kim and Mauborgne's (2003) *Harvard Business Review* article 'Tipping Point Leadership' can be useful when bringing strategy to life using their four-step approach:

1. Break through the cognitive hurdle. Help your audience to experience the problem rather than consider it as abstract. Storytelling is a helpful technique to use here; gather real examples of the problems or customer needs that are creating the need to change.
2. Sidestep the resource hurdle (choose your battles). This is about focusing resources on the areas of change that will make the biggest difference first. Don't try to achieve everything at once; identify some quick wins and deliver them. Jump the motivational hurdle.
3. Identify key influencers within the business who can change the organization for you. Consider the ripple effect if you drop a stone into a pool of water. Knock over the political hurdle.

4. Even when change is about to take place and the tipping point is reached there will still be resistors or saboteurs who want to cling on to the old way. Identify these people up front, particularly if they're senior, and have the courage to involve them and get them on board.[7]

Connecting with strategy is about creating the 'why' for change; it gives people the vision and motivation to want to change, and it also sets key milestones and goals that keep the change on track.

So what? Over to you…

1. How does the change you're leading connect to your organization's wider strategy? What does that mean for the story you're telling?

Connecting with strategy

2. What are the relevant PESTLE factors, and are you explaining those well enough?

3. What milestones or goals would be most helpful to set along the way?

Day 3
Corroboration

Change is so much easier when people don't feel coerced or pressured into having to change against their will. Effective Change Agents understand how to use non-manipulative persuasive skills to provide the rationale for change.

Shortcuts to influence

In his book *Influence: The Psychology of Persuasion*, Robert Cialdini outlines six shortcuts that we use as the basis for making decisions: authority, consensus, consistency, liking, reciprocity and scarcity. Let's look at each one in turn.[8]

Authority

In this context we're referring to validation of a course of action by a relevant and highly regarded or powerful authority such as the CEO of an organization or external authorities (industry experts, governments or regulatory bodies).

This is change compliance and is not the same as buy-in; it's more a case of reluctant acceptance. Let's look at other more positive motivators, like those below, to encourage greater buy-in.

Consensus or social proof

Our need for consensus probably stems from our innate human instinct to be part of a group. This is related to a concept called social proof, where we seek assurance that others have also bought into an idea before making the decision to buy in ourselves. As with authority, we seek social proof from people (remember 'the First Follower'?) or businesses like us. So to influence using social proof, we might use examples of other organizations in a similar industry or a similar customer who applied this change strategy successfully.

It's amazing how often we're influenced by or rely on social proof: think about the power of

TripAdvisor or Amazon reviews. And the more we identify with the person providing the reference or recommendation, the more likely we are to be influenced by it.

Consistency

We like to think we're consistent; if we say 'yes' to something small, we're more likely to say 'yes' to something similar but bigger in the future.

So in a business context, if we want to make changes to working hours we might ask people to make a small adjustment in hours initially and then increase this over time. It's important, though, that people don't feel manipulated.

People tend to focus on what's changing, so it can be helpful to remind them of what's staying the same. They may have a change in manager, but it's the same job, with the same colleagues, in the same office with the same hours and the same commute, for example.

Liking

If people like us, they're more likely to listen to us and trust us. But this isn't simple. We tend to like people we consider similar to us, and we decide whether we like people through unconscious things such as body language, eye contact and whether we believe they're interested in and like *us*. So how can you become more likeable?

- Ask for feedback from friends or colleagues. Is your body language consistently friendly, or do you sometimes come across as defensive, evasive or closed?
- Consider how good you are at taking a genuine interest in other people. Do you ask them open questions? Do you listen carefully to their responses and build on them? Or do you jump around, change the subject or perhaps not ask many questions at all?
- Go out of your way to find things you have in common (which means asking questions and being interested in their answers). Finding common ground is a key skill when building rapport and trust.
- A quick way of building rapport is by finding something to compliment about someone. It must be sincere and not too personal in the workplace, not 'you look hot in that shirt', more 'I really liked the way you handled that difficult question that James asked'.

Corroboration

- Humour or self-deprecation can build rapport with a larger audience. When we laugh together, we bond together, and we feel warmly towards the person who made us laugh.

Reciprocity or exchange

Exchange is linked to the well-known reciprocation principle: if you give someone something, even of low value, the recipient naturally feels an obligation to reciprocate or give something back. Offering a concession will increase the chances of the other side also making a concession.

In the context of change, this could be enhancements to a redundancy package, such as garden leave or support in finding a new job. Of course, you need to understand people's actual expectations before you know whether they'll see an offer as positive!

Scarcity

Scarcity is a frequently used marketing ploy; 'buy now, before it's too late'. It could also be used in change management; for example, by offering a small number of voluntary redundancies within a certain time frame.

Do Change Better

Most of us will accept the need for change more readily if we experience a range of persuasive reasons to buy in. Change is more likely to stick if people choose to change rather than feeling coerced.

✏️ So what? Over to you...

1. Which of those six principles of influence feels most important for you to master right now, and why?

Corroboration

2. How can you increase your likeability to increase your ability to lead change? Are there any particular relationships you need to work on?

3. How can you ensure that you're persuasive without being manipulative?

Day 4

Communication and collaboration

Communication

The ability to build trust effectively is a key skill for a Change Agent and this involves listening more than we speak and making sure that our non-verbal communication aligns with our verbal messaging.

John Kotter, a Harvard professor and renowned expert on large-scale business change, says that we rarely communicate frequently or effectively enough about business change, in fact he suggests that change should be communicated 10 times more than we think it should be. Successful Change Agents understand that *how* we communicate is just as important as *how often* we communicate.

More than what we say: understanding how we communicate

In the 1960s, Albert Meharabian (1981) identified that the words we use can represent a very small proportion of the meaning *that's taken* from communication.[9] Our tone of voice, facial expressions and body language carry more weight with listeners if they're not aligned with the words we're using.

So as Change Agents, it's important to rehearse the *way* we deliver a message in terms of tonality and body language, particularly if we have strong personal feelings about the change. If we're not comfortable about the message, our tone of voice and body language could well give this away. It's helpful for us to be aware of the potential impact of our own unconscious idiosyncrasies.

Facial expressions and body language include behaviours such as posture. Are my arms or legs crossed or open? Do I use particular hand gestures or tilt my head in a certain way? Facially, are my brows raised or lowered? Do I furrow my brows, hold eye contact or look away?

Communication and collaboration

We communicate emotions through our vocal intonation, levels of inflection, pitch and pace. For example, we may speak more quickly when we're excited or nervous. Having a lower-pitched voice is commonly interpreted as being more authoritative. British Prime Minister Margaret Thatcher famously underwent voice coaching to lower the pitch of her voice in order to sound more authoritative.

Rapport

Rapport is a shared understanding or state of mutual trust, and it's a huge help when we're communicating difficult messages. Mirroring and matching – unconsciously copying other people's body language and mannerisms and repeating their words – helps build trust and establishes rapport.

Matching usually has a built-in 'time lag'. For example, if the person we're communicating with uncrosses their legs and leans slightly inward while speaking, we might wait for a few seconds and then discreetly adopt the same posture.

But if we're listening to someone in a rage, we obviously don't want to match their anger back at them because emotions will escalate and effective communication will go out of the window. Instead, we'll need to mismatch (which will break rapport) or try something more subtle: pacing and leading. This is where we may gain or maintain rapport by reflecting the tempo of the communication; for example, nodding slightly in time with the pace of the language then gradually slowing down, leading the other person to become calmer.

As you might imagine, behaviours that mismatch are more likely to damage rapport and break trust between individuals. I've found that one of the best ways of delivering messages around change is to ensure that my thoughts about my message are positive and I'm clear about what the change is and why we're making it.

Meta-programs

Rodger Bailey created a model called the Language and Behaviour Profile, identifying a set of patterns, called meta-programs, that are based on our own experiences, background and disposition.

These meta-programs are context-specific and are not the same as personality preferences. When we understand how someone is motivated, we can tailor our language to make it more influential. There are many categories of meta-program, but the following three are most relevant to us as Change Agents.

Towards versus away motivation

This is where a person is motivated *towards* a goal or *away* from pain. When we're thinking about motivating others to change we need to have both 'towards' and 'away' language in our communications kitbag to ensure that the change message appeals to everyone. 'Towards' language may be about painting the picture of an exciting new future, whereas an 'away' message would be more about avoiding the pain of an undesirable current or future situation.

Best-case- versus worst-case-scenario thinking

What do you focus on first – positive opportunities and possibilities, or risks and potential threats?

Working with people who look for positive possibilities is easier in terms of initial buy-in than those who look for the worst case when rolling out change. But it can be helpful to have someone who considers the worst-case scenario in order to spot potential risks up front and plan for them. Having a group of optimistic best-case thinkers can be unrealistic and set us up for failure.

Similarities versus differences

As Change Agents, we can reassure people by highlighting all the things that are staying the same within a situation to keep the areas of change or difference proportionate. For example, we may be moving offices, which involves a different commute to work and different desk, etc. However, we will still have the same working hours, manager and team.

Learned filters

Much of this thinking comes from a branch of psychology called NLP – Neuro-Linguistic Programming. Another NLP theory is that there are three learned filters, or shortcuts, through which we view the world: deletion, distortion and generalization.

Deletion

This is when we unconsciously ignore certain pieces of information in order to reinforce our existing view of the world. In a change situation, this may mean we don't 'hear' certain pieces of information. If we believe that the company doesn't care about its people, we won't 'hear' how it's trying to do its best for them.

Distortion

This is when we take reality and twist it. Someone who's been objectively placed into a group 'at risk' of redundancy might say, 'I knew that they didn't like me.' To respond, you could keep returning to the facts, ideally with evidence; for example, 'I know HR had the redundancy criteria and assessments checked for objectivity, so I'm sure nothing is personal.'

Generalization

This is a bit like distortion, but the application is broader – 'This sort of thing always happens.' The best way to deal with other people's generalizations is to ask for specifics; for example, 'Who's had special treatment?' Usually it becomes clear that there are really just a couple of examples, and this allows us to put the generalization into context.

Empathic listening

Communication is also about how we listen and what we hear. It's a two-way process. Listening appropriately means taking the words on board, listening to the tone of voice and observing the body language that others use, to recognize the attitudes or emotions behind the communication. As Change Agents, it's our job to show that we've *really* heard the message that others are portraying, even if that message is non-verbal.

'Active listening' is when we listen hard to what the other person is saying, nod our head, make eye contact and demonstrate positive body language. But active listening can come across as confrontational in some circumstances; for example, when emotions are high. This is when empathic listening is most helpful as a skill to develop and use.

Stephen Covey defines empathic listening as the highest form of listening in his best-selling business book *The 7 Habits of Highly Effective People*.[10] He explains that the purpose is *not* listening until we understand, but listening until the other person feels understood. He named this 'emotional oxygen', giving people the chance to breathe and relax.

Empathic listening may simply include using non-words such as 'mmmhmm'. Obviously, our body language and facial expressions demonstrate our wish to understand. By allowing the other person to truly express how they feel we can truly understand the root of the problem. So, unlike active listening, it's good to restrain ourselves from asking probing questions until the emotion has subsided. Instead, it's better to reflect empathically the emotions that we believe the person is demonstrating; for example, 'That sounds frustrating?' Notice the question mark at the end of the statement; that's important because we can't be sure of the person's emotion. Empathic listening doesn't usually need to be used for long – just while emotions are high. Once things are calmer we can move to more active listening and problem-solving.

Collaboration

Change Agents, however effective, can't deliver organizational change on their own – they need to encourage everyone working together to collaborate and go in the same direction.

Simply put, collaboration is two or more people working together to achieve a common goal. It's about always looking for ways in which people can benefit by working together across roles and silos.

Defining collaboration

My definition, for this purpose, is a tribe of like-minded individuals with complementary skills, all of whom are committed to do what it takes to deliver the change – our very own Change League, each with their own talents and strengths but sharing the same end goal.

People who are collaborative demonstrate open, positive body language. They have the EI to read the reactions of those around them when they're responding to a certain idea or situation and involve them when gathering feedback. This may be by asking open questions such as: 'What do you think about that idea?' Or it may involve a gentle challenge; for example, 'You don't look so keen on that idea?'

The naturally collaborative Change Agent builds trust because they're clearly focused on achieving the most positive possible outcome for all concerned. They're unselfishly looking for a win/win solution to any problem and are *genuinely* interested in the wants and needs of others: 'What could we do that would make this change better for your team?'

Collaboration breeds goodwill and trust. It's the secret ingredient, the glue that binds everything together. Let's break it down into the five key collaborative skills.

Being open-minded

We can't *not* communicate. Our body language is always providing clues to the way we feel about a person or situation. So, as Change Agents, we begin by working on our mindset. There are two aspects to this:

1. Even if we don't like a change to start with, we need to understand the reasons and come to terms with the rationale for it. We need to feel genuinely open-minded about the potential positive benefits of the change and be prepared to communicate those benefits.
2. We need to be open-minded about the reactions and behaviours of others that we interact with when managing change. Much of this will come from our understanding the way different personalities naturally respond to change.

Being open-minded takes self-discipline and patience, especially if the other person doesn't appear to be cooperating. It's important to not provide energy or reinforcement for their negative behaviour. Collaborative people are all about the positive ripples that build up to make a bigger difference, but sometimes it's not about the transmission of positive energy; sometimes it's about choosing not to transmit negative energy.

Interpersonal awareness

We also need to be great at reading the behaviours of others. Sometimes we may notice someone nod as if they agree, but their facial expression or tone of voice conveys a different message. As Change Agents we need to have the courage to spot this lack of congruence or alignment in the way others are communicating and be prepared to challenge it. (Congruence is when our body language and tone of voice convey the same message; incongruence is when an aspect of our communication, usually body language, tone of voice or facial expression, conveys a different message to our actual words, e.g. frowning while nodding our head as if in agreement.)

Consider the most likely response to this question: 'Are you sure that you're happy to go along with this?' This is a closed and slightly leading question, so it's most likely that the individual will just answer 'yes', rather than opening themselves up to be challenged.

But you could follow it up with an open question: 'I can see you're nodding, but your facial expression gives me the impression that you're not 100% convinced. What else could we discuss to ensure that you're completely happy?'

The person may reply: 'No, I'm on board – I'm just squinting because the sun's in my eyes,' in which case, great! More likely, though, they'll feel like they have permission to talk about their concerns, which gives us a chance to address something that may have gone on to become an obstacle later.

Notice that I used a 'what' or open question, which requires more than a 'yes' or 'no' response. Using 'what' here implies that the individual has questions, so they feel more able to ask them.

Positive communication

Open questions that require more than a 'yes' or 'no' response are positive, as long as our body language gives the impression that we genuinely want to know the answer to the questions that we ask. Try smiling as you ask a question or making sure that your internal mindset is genuinely positive or at least neutral to avoid any non-verbal 'tells'. If people start explaining their concerns, make sure your body language remains open and doesn't appear defensive. This means strong eye contact and avoiding crossing your arms or legs if possible. Use of the word 'we' is powerful because it automatically creates the impression that you're both on the same team, rather than creating a position of opposition that may make people defensive.

Flexibility

Being collaborative requires us to be able to use our interpersonal awareness to spot how others are feeling and to have the flexibility to adjust our own behaviours, verbal responses or body language to build rapport and to be the most appropriate for the situation. Once we have rapport by matching the appropriate behaviours, we may be able to change the tempo or tone of communication and take the other person with us emotionally.

We can only achieve this if we have the flexibility to notice behaviours and match them, gaining rapport and trust before we gradually adjust the tone or tempo. This is very subtle and effective if done well by a flexible communicator with a positive intent and mindset.

Comfort with ambiguity

During change the future becomes uncertain, which can mean people feel blocked or unable to move forwards. Change Agents who can create small pockets of certainty (e.g. by setting short-term goals) in an ambiguous situation provide reassurance, helping people to move forwards.

Communication and collaboration

The key is for us to make the best decision based on the information we have, and to be prepared to change direction in future if needed as we find out more.

> ### ✏️ So what? Over to you...
>
> 1. Are there situations in which your communication might be compromised by your mindset, body language or lack of rapport? What might you do about that?

2. Look back at those three 'learned filters': deletion, distortion and generalization. Which of these feels most relevant to you right now, and why?

Communication and collaboration

3. Which of those five key collaboration skills do you most need to work on right now?

Day 5
Change and personality

The better we understand how personalities and predictable emotional responses affect individual behaviour during change, the easier it is for us to react appropriately.

Personalities, styles and strategies

Internal and external 'loci of control' are the extents to which individuals feel they can control or are responsible for the events that take place in their lives.

- Internal locus of control: people have a greater sense that they can effect change themselves. (People with an internal locus of control have been shown to have more positive reactions to organizational change.)

- External locus of control: people tend to feel things are done to them.

As Change Agents we can help people focus on the aspects of the change that they control. Involvement in the planning and roll-out of change is a great way to empower people to feel more positive about it. Remember, it's not always the case that people dislike change; it's more the case that they dislike change being 'done to them'.

Organizational changes can cause stress, depression, uncertainty and insecurity. Various factors cause stress at different stages of change. Before a change, main stress factors might be workload, limited resources and too much or too little responsibility. During change they might be uncertainty, unclear roles or lack of consultation/participations. And after change they might shift to workload, inadequate resources and uncertainty. Relationships, both internal and external, tend to be a source of stress at every stage!

The transition curve

The 'transition curve' originated from the work of Elisabeth Kübler-Ross (1969), who studied how people coped with death and bereavement.[11]

Organizational change can be considered a form of loss, even if the final outcome is positive.

Kübler-Ross identified seven or eight stages and emotions that people go through during bereavement, ranging from shock and depression to integration. I'm going to use an adapted version of the transition curve that's helpful in business. There are just four stages to this journey, as can be seen in the figure below.

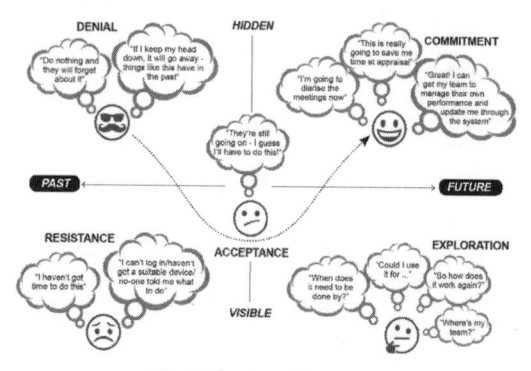

Fig. 1 The transition curve

The four stages that people typically go through are:

1. Denial
2. Resistance
3. Exploration
4. Commitment

Change and personality

Depending on the desirability of the change, it's possible to go through each stage almost instantaneously, or at a snail's pace. It's also possible to move backwards and forwards along the curve. Each stage of the transition curve brings its own set of emotions and behaviours.

Of course, the goal for us as Change Agents is to support people as they move through the curve so that they reach commitment in the shortest time possible, and stay there.

Denial

We're creatures of habit and drawn towards equilibrium; denial is a great way to avoid 'rocking the boat', by hoping that the proposed change will just go away.

Being in denial is effective for people who don't like change. It's easy to mistake silent denial for commitment and wrongly assume that someone is on board with the change because they're not saying otherwise. The effective Change Agent doesn't allow this to happen; they spot the possible denial and encourage the individual to express their feelings by asking specific and open questions about their views.

This allows them to manage any concerns and move around the change curve.

Resistance

We can recognize resistance in this context when we hear statements like 'this will never work' or 'I've seen it all before'. The Change Agent needs to use their empathic listening skills to truly understand the individual's concerns and encourage them to continue to speak.

It's vital to let people speak without interruption. We can help by using open questions such as: 'Can you tell me a bit more about your concerns around the changes to your working hours?'

When Change Agents continue to listen effectively, the individual will start to move through the curve by themselves. They'll begin to ask questions that are more future-orientated, even if they still appear a little hostile. They might say something like, 'Who's going to handle all the extra work caused by this change?' Although these are still slightly resistant questions, they're more positive and future-orientated, and are a sign that the individual is starting to progress towards the next stage of exploration.

Change and personality

Exploration

Exploration is an equally vocal stage where people interact and question the future vision, looking for possibilities. For example, 'Will I get a pay rise?' or 'What new roles will be available?'

The main difference between resistance and exploration is the fact that the individual is clearly starting to picture what the future will look like after the change has taken place and they tend to be more positive. Remember, even as Change Agents we don't have to know all the answers immediately; what we need to do is understand the concerns fully and ensure that people feel heard. It's then perfectly okay to say that you're going to take the issues away in order to get full answers. We're then able to group concerns together, use them to inform future communication and provide more comprehensive answers.

This exercise allows people to express their views and concerns in a safe, non-judgemental way that helps them to process the change. Even without providing answers, we're helping them come to terms with the change – just as in the grieving process.

Some people will naturally move from exploration to commitment on their own, particularly if they believe it to be positive. Some, though, will remain stuck, even when we've answered their questions to the best of our ability.

Figure 2 illustrates how we can help people through each stage of the transition curve.

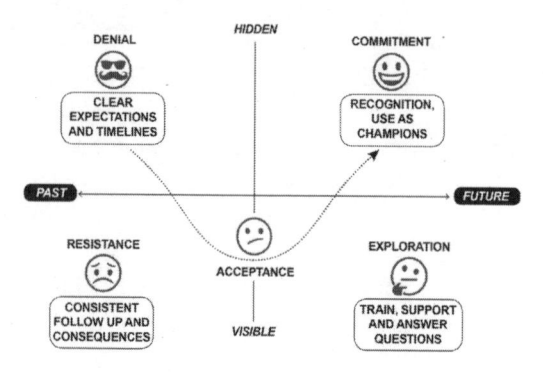

Fig. 2 How to manage each stage

Commitment

By the commitment stage the frantic questions have ceased and the energy becomes more channelled. But be careful not to mistake the quietness of denial for the quietness of commitment. Ask a few questions about how they feel about the change. If you get a quick and positive answer, then they've reached commitment. But if they take a deep breath and give a textbook answer, or their body language appears

Change and personality

incongruent, then you may need to ask a few follow-up questions to be truly sure that they're on board.

If we're to be successful in delivering change then we must take as many people with us, as quickly as possible. People who have made it through the Change Curve and reached commitment are in a great position to help others through the same journey. They may become our First Followers, early adopters or champions – all key roles during organizational change.

One of the worst things that can happen is if people 'quit and stay': they don't buy in to the change but they don't choose to vote with their feet and leave. In organizations where successive changes have taken place but haven't been driven through to completion there can be a high proportion of people who fit into this category, creating a culture of resistance and stagnation. By understanding each individual, one at a time, you can unblock stagnant cultures, increasing the chances of a successful change outcome.

Personality

Everyone is unique and personalities vary, as do responses to change. Individual differences or personalities can often cause misunderstanding or conflict, particularly during change.

Myers–Briggs type indicator

The Myers–Briggs Type Indicator (MBTI) is a well known personality tool and can be a helpful framework in the context of change. Its origins can be traced back to original research by psychologist Carl Jung in the 1920s, developed over 40 years by Briggs and Myers.

MBTI uses four different dimensions of type, referred to by single letters. These dichotomies are classified as follows:

1. Where you focus your attention – extroversion (E) or introversion (I)
2. How you take in information – sensing (S) or intuition (N)
3. How you make decisions – thinking (T) or feeling (F)
4. How you deal with the world – judging (J) or perceiving (P)

When using MBTI one to one, we typically group the dimensions together to give someone a four-letter type (e.g. ENTP or ISTJ). However, those types can

Extroversion or introversion

Extroversion and introversion can often, but not always, be recognized by how expressive someone is about their internal thoughts.

Think back to the transition curve. It's likely that extroverts are going to express their feelings about change sooner than introverts. It's also likely that we'll have a disproportionate input of views from the extroverts, who are more likely to express their feelings voluntarily, than we do from the introverts. This could result in a distorted picture.

An introvert may be in the resistance stage of the transition curve in their head but may not express it. The risk is that a Change Agent hears extroverts talking excitedly about the future and they assume that everybody's on board. Extroverts can be very vocal and dominant and in an emotive environment of change this could mean that we only get to hear their side of the story; we need to hear from both types of people.

This means accepting that introverts may take longer to process information and to share how they feel, and we need to create safe environments that allow them to do that.

Sensing or intuition

A sensing preference is characterized by a preference for more practical, detailed processes, whereas intuition is more vague, futuristic and 'big-picture'. Someone with a sensing preference likes lots of structured information. They want to understand the process step-by-step before they move forwards. These are the sort of people who may seem to be stuck at the resistance stage of the transition curve because they're questioning all the facts. But when we realize this is just how they process the world, and provide them with the detail they need, then they'll happily move on.

Thinking or feeling

Someone with a thinking preference presented with a potentially emotive change such as redundancy is likely to just accept it, if they believe it's supported by a logical rationale. But someone with a feeling preference makes decisions based on values and

Change and personality

feelings. In the same situation they'll often be concerned for other people, not just themselves, and may appear quite emotional.

As Change Agents we need to respond appropriately to both these styles, treating people fairly in any change situation. A Change Agent with a thinking preference may be very matter-of-fact about change, which could appear cold. But someone delivering change with a feeling preference may bring too much emotion to their communication. Both risks can be avoided with self-awareness.

Judging or perceiving

It's important to understand that judging doesn't mean being judgemental in this context – it simply means that people like closure. Those with a judging preference like to make decisions and have plans and structures agreed. They also like to have time to plan, and don't appreciate last-minute changes.

People with a perceiving preference like to leave their options open, are flexible and tend to see a change of plan as an opportunity. They seek out change and are likely to move quickly through the transformation curve to the exploration stage, looking for the positives that the change may bring. (In my experience, people with a perceiving preference are also likely to be natural Change Agents.)

Delivering change effectively requires us to take the majority with us, and developing the ability to understand and communicate in line with individual differences is another way of doing this.

✎ So what? Over to you...

1. How do you see the transition curve playing out in your organization?

Change and personality

2. How might your own MBTI type help and hinder you as you lead change?

3. Think about someone you particularly need to communicate well with. How might their preferences differ from yours, and what does that mean for your communication style?

Day 6
Cultures, values and leadership

However well thought out the technical and project-related aspects of change, Change Agents can still encounter insurmountable resistance if they don't address its cultural aspects.

Cultural models

'Onion Model'

One particularly useful model here is Edgar Schein's (1984) 'Onion Model'.[12] He divided culture into three different levels:

1. Symbols and artefacts

2. Espoused values
3. Basic underlying assumptions

I've adapted his model here to show how closely interlinked leadership and values are when it comes to recognizing culture.

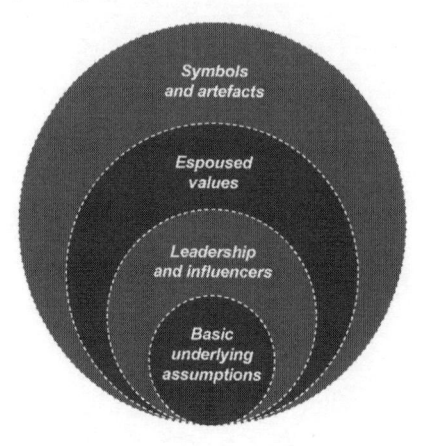

Fig. 3 The 'Onion Model'

Symbols and artefacts

The outside layer of culture is demonstrated through symbols and artefacts such as logos, branding, corporate offices, job titles, hierarchies and some processes. Formal examples may be recognition schemes or a company website. Less formal examples may be the way people dress or communicate when making decisions.

The modern symbols and artefacts of many of the highly successful software firms in Silicon Valley, such as bright décor, beanbags and pool tables, are synonymous with a young, innovative culture. Other companies have introduced similar features in the hope of emulating the success of these businesses, only to realize that they're just symbols of the culture, not its cause. Simply changing a logo or brand or making other symbolic changes is not the same as actual culture change – that needs to originate from within the deeper layers of an organization. It's the leadership behaviours and espoused values of the company that drive the creativity and innovation, not the table football or indoor deckchairs.

Espoused values

Values are the core beliefs and commitments that underpin the way a company conducts business. Every company has values – they're recognizable through the behaviours that are demonstrated daily and are particularly visible in the actions of leaders and key influencers.

Sometimes these values are baked into a company from the start by its founders. Sometimes they evolve over time as a company grows and differentiates itself from the competition. Values can establish behavioural standards and help employees make the right decisions in the absence of specific guidance.

As a company grows, it's important that these values also evolve so that they reflect the culture we aspire to, rather than the culture we used to have. Schein calls them primary embedding mechanisms:

- What we measure on a regular basis – think dashboards and KPIs.
- The way emergencies or critical incidents are handled.
- The way resources are allocated.
- The behaviours that are role-modelled, recognized and encouraged by leaders.
- The allocation of reward and promotion.

Leadership and influencers

Many values-based change initiatives are received with cynicism, particularly if they're perceived to be imposed from the top down or leaders are seen as paying 'lip service' to them. The bottom line is that the behaviours of the leaders and managers will reinforce or undermine any defined values and in turn make or break any culture change.

Basic underlying assumptions

According to the Onion Model, unconscious behaviours or beliefs tend to be so deep-rooted that they're hard to recognize from within the organization or in an individual, but new starters may find them noticeable. For example, a new starter coming to a start-up from a corporate background might expect a formal induction, but find they're expected to learn 'on the job' with minimal training.

Takeaways

Schein's model implies that making changes from the inside out, rather than the outside in, is the way forward. Basic assumptions may be too deep-rooted to change, but leadership and values are a better place to start.

An organization's culture will almost certainly have developed over time, possibly as a response to external market forces. A business may have developed a culture of being fast-moving and innovative to take advantage of technology. On the other hand, a business in a very highly regulated marketplace may appear to be risk-averse and focused on quality. If market forces change, we may need to behave in ways that are counter to our culture to be more competitive.

Earlier, we talked about connecting with strategy. Making the link with market forces helps everyone to understand why the change is necessary and motivates people to move in a new direction.

The Competing Values Framework

From their research into what makes organizations effective, Robert Quinn and Kim Cameron came up with the Competing Values Framework.[13] They identified two dimensions: flexibility versus stability, and internal versus external orientation, which resulted in four quadrants with distinctly different corporate cultures, as shown in Figure 4.

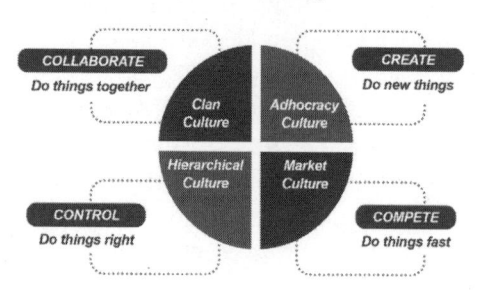

Fig. 4 Competing Values Framework

Cultures, values and leadership

Clan culture

Culture is built on personal relationships or loyalty, particularly to the founder or clan leader. The company may be referred to as having a 'family feel', which may be positive, although as with families there can be infighting and bickering too. The organizational values are likely to be disproportionately affected by the personal values or behavioural style of the founder or family, which can be problematic as the company grows and wants to scale up or sell.

Our role as Change Agents here is to hold a mirror up to the clan leader's behaviours if they aren't supporting the new way of working.

Hierarchical culture

In hierarchical cultures the prevailing values are 'do things right' and 'follow the rules' because these provide stability and control, resulting in quality and efficiency. The challenge for this culture is speed to adapt to change. Risk-averse, hierarchical cultures can be slow to change, which could ultimately affect their ability to survive. The hierarchical businesses that do well are those that manage to 'bake in' innovation as part of their processes and values.

Market culture

Market cultures are focused on goals and results, and clearly align themselves with the external marketplace. They aim to predict and respond to customer needs to beat the competition, achieving profitability and market dominance. Change in this culture needs to be strongly aligned with the company strategy and it's likely that the culture is set by a handful of key influencers, particularly in sales and marketing. Winning over key individuals for any culture change will therefore be essential.

Adhocracy culture

We often hear the term 'disruptive' being applied to businesses that are shaking up traditional marketplaces through innovation. They may be winning business from traditional hierarchical cultures or they may be creating new markets. They value creativity and speed to market, which means the management style needs to be empowering so that people feel able to take the initiative.

Power may not necessarily sit with those who are most senior. Individuals with key technical skills can be extremely powerful and change can be initiated or resisted from anywhere in the organization.

The Cultural Web

At the core of Johnson, Scholes and Whittington's Cultural Web (1999) is the organizational paradigm: the core values, mindset or motivation of the organization.[14]

Fig. 5 The Cultural Web

- **Organizational structures.** The hierarchy of the organization that shows where the power

lies, how decisions are made and where communication flows.
- **Control systems.** The systems and mechanisms that report on and control the organization.
- **Power structures.** The people and systems that have power and influence and can get things done, with both formal positional power and informal personal power.
- **Symbols.** The official and unofficial visual representations of culture (e.g. logos, offices, uniforms).
- **Stories and myths.** Past events and stories about the organization and its people that continue to be shared both internally and externally.
- **Rituals and routines.** The habitual activities, norms and ways of working.

We can use this model to analyse our current culture – 'as is' – and to help define the culture that is 'to be'. This helps provide clarity about the required change, both structural and cultural, which helps us decide what changes need to be made to embed it.

Cultures, values and leadership

An example of a cultural web

	As is	To be
Organizational paradigm	Financially stable, trustworthy, quality- and research-driven	Innovative, responsive, customer-focused
Organizational structures	Hierarchical roles with formal reporting into a parent company	Matrix or team-based structures focused around market requirements
Control systems	Board of directors and non-execs make decisions. Formal annual cycles of budgeting, headcount and objective cascade	Disseminated decision-making and financial controls and business-case-driven resourcing and budgeting
Power structures	CEO and CFO and influence of the parent company	Individual empowerment and accountability with local team leaders and managers
Symbols	Traditional brand and logo, parking spaces for top execs, status related to size of office and formal business attire at work	Open-plan buildings, hot desks, 'chill-out zones' and online collaboration tools

Rituals and routines	Annual business planning, board meetings, sales conferences, annual reports and long-service awards	Team huddles, weekly one-to-ones, informal Skype chats and fish-and-chip Fridays
Stories and myths	The CFO values the company car fleet above people, there's gossip about the executive board, and board meetings never finish on time	Reward and recognition linked to customer impact, innovation suggestion schemes and individual success stories

Culture is one of the biggest causes of conflict in managing change, so let's end Day 6 by taking a look at what that might mean and how to manage it.

Conflict

There are two main types of conflict: overt and covert.

Overt conflict

Overt conflict is visible; it's when people display emotions. The reasons for overt conflict may be fear, lack of understanding or the other person just having a bad day. Whatever the cause, the solution is the same – we must listen and show *sincere* empathy for the emotions being displayed. Sincere, empathic listening involves eye contact, nodding, a sympathetic facial expression and occasional reflective statements such as: 'That must have been extremely frustrating.' We need to make the other person feel understood, and when their response to our reflective statement is an impassioned 'yes!', we know people will be more open to our views or recommendations.

Overt challenge can be intimidating, but there's also a more insidious type of conflict that can be just as challenging, and possibly more damaging if not addressed.

Covert conflict

In covert conflict, people don't air their concerns openly, so it can be hard to spot. We might recognize incongruent body language where someone agrees to a change or action but their facial expression doesn't align with the spoken words. They may demonstrate a blank facial expression, quietly shake their heads or shrug when you're delivering a message. We might notice them mouthing words under their breath or whispering to someone next to them. It's very easy to ignore or overlook these behaviours, particularly if we'd rather avoid direct conflict personally but – unchecked – they can result in the spread of negativity and resistance to the change.

To deal with covert conflict, our tone of voice and facial expression need to be curious rather than combative; for example, 'All views are valid and welcome; what are your thoughts on this suggestion?' Reinforce the fact that you're open to all views and that the change is here to stay, so it's important that everyone is on board.

So what? Over to you…

1. What are the 'symbols and artefacts' that reveal your organization's underlying assumptions, and what does that reveal to you about managing culture change?

Cultures, values and leadership

2. Which of the four 'competing values' quadrants best captures your current culture? What does that reveal to you about managing culture change in your organization?

3. How well equipped are you to handle both overt and covert conflict? How can you strengthen that capability?

Day 7

Build your change league

We don't have to 'do change' alone – in fact we really can't. By building a League of Change Champions, we can draw on different individual strengths at the optimum time.

The best-known model of successful teams was discovered by Meredith Belbin and his team in the 1960s and published in a book called *Management Teams* (2010).[15] They noticed that people tended to take on certain behaviours and activities when they were in a team. Belbin grouped these into nine clusters of behaviour and called them 'team roles', defined as 'a tendency to behave, contribute and interrelate with others in a particular way'. This research proposed that each team would need to have access to all nine behaviours in order to be high-performing, although not necessarily all at the same time.

You don't need nine people for an effective team; most people can take on two or three team roles comfortably. As is the case with personality types, each role has its own strengths as well as what Belbin termed 'allowable weaknesses' – the natural downside or opposite of a strength.

Appreciating the pros and cons of each role in forming an effective team helps us to understand the cause of competition rather than collaboration in a team. By looking across the spread of roles on a project we can predict where we may succeed or fail based on the natural composition of the team. This gives us the option to bring in additional team members with the missing strengths or to ask someone already in the team to take on a certain role instead. While we may never be as good at that role, or perhaps enjoy it as much, as someone who has it as a natural strength, having the awareness and intention to take it on for the benefit of the overall team can make a huge difference.

Let's look at the nine different roles and when they're most useful. I've outlined them below in the order that they tend to be most useful within a project.

Build your change league

At the beginning of a change or project

Shaper

This role is usually filled by someone who is assertive, confident and outspoken. Shapers challenge the team to improve, deliver on time and provide a sense of urgency. They're good at getting started, overcoming obstacles and are goal-oriented. Shapers are good at cutting through confusion and steering a path.

Allowable weakness

Shapers may be blunt and their goal orientation can be seen as argumentative. It's important that they utilize other, more people-orientated strengths such as listening and empathy when communicating change to others.

Resource investigator

Resource investigators are optimistic, enthusiastic and naturally collaborative. They're quick to act and great at exploring options and solutions or negotiating for resources. At the start of a project or change, their enthusiasm is contagious, making them skilled at winning over cynics and influencing stakeholders.

Allowable weakness

Once their initial enthusiasm wears off, the resource investigator can lose interest or become distracted by the next project. They may forget to finish things or overlook details.

Coordinator

Coordinators are more individualistic. They take on the traditional team-leader role, agreeing specific objectives, delegating tasks and guiding the team to achieve the desired outcome. They're calm and understand the individual strengths of each team member.

Allowable weakness

Coordinators can sometimes be seen as manipulative or be resented for excessive delegation.

During the change or project

Implementer

Implementers turn ideas and concepts into action. They're practical, systematic and disciplined. They're reliable and well organized and can be counted on to follow the plan and achieve their goals. While implementers may need to be won over initially in response to a change, once on board they're highly loyal and committed.

Allowable weakness

Because they like to follow a plan, implementers can be seen as inflexible or uninspiring.

Teamworker

Teamworkers are *people* people. They're harmonious and supportive and will work cooperatively with others in the best interests of the team. They tend to be flexible, diplomatic and good at reading the emotions of others. This makes them good communicators and they display high levels of empathy. Teamworkers are useful at all stages of a project because of their flexibility. They fit well in the middle and towards the end of a project when individuals are comfortable in their roles.

Allowable weakness

Their desire to get on with others can make them shy away from conflict and they may seem indecisive or unwilling to take a clear position during team discussions.

Plant

Plants tends to be creative, full of ideas and good at solving complex problems. They can be introverted, so may need to be encouraged to share their thoughts. Their skills can be useful at the start of a project when brainstorming initial ideas, or in the middle of a project when obstacles may have arisen.

Allowable weakness

They may be poor communicators or too quiet to speak up. Sometimes, their ideas may be impractical or too abstract to use.

Specialist

The Specialist role was added later by Belbin. The specialist is a technical expert and they may be required at any stage during a change.

Allowable weakness

Specialists may appear hung up on technicalities or may be considered intimidating. Depending on their other team roles they can seem less committed to the overall team.

Build your change league

At the end of the change or project

Monitor evaluator

Monitor evaluators are great at analysing and evaluating ideas that others have come up with and will often spot problems before they arise. Clearly, this skill makes them useful throughout the change, not just at the end. However, because they're critical thinkers and think hard before they act, they're often more visible towards the end of a project. They also have a keen eye for quality so come into their own when the shapers and resource investigators try to cut corners or lose interest.

Allowable weakness

Sometimes accused of 'analysis paralysis', they can get bogged down in small details or be accused of slowing things down.

Completer finisher

Completer finishers ensure the project is seen through to the end, dotting the 'i's, crossing the 't's and ensuring that there are no errors or omissions. They're very focused on meeting deadlines, so if a project has been well structured with regular milestones, they'll also keep the team on track along the way. They're conscientious, orderly and thorough.

Allowable weakness

Because of the focus on perfectionism, this role may be seen as overly critical and a bit of a worrier.

Remember, we're all able to take on any role if we have to, and we all have at least two roles that come quite naturally to us. It's better to bring in someone with a natural strength rather than force someone to take on a role that they find difficult.

Build a balanced team with good representation across all nine roles. It's perfectly fine to give someone else the role of team leader for the purpose of delivering the project, even if you're the most senior person in the team. You don't want a team of clones with people playing roles that are outside of their comfort zone.

The stages of building a high-performing team

Be aware of the different stages that each team goes through in the process of building towards high performance. Tuckman's team development theory

Build your change league

(1965) explains this, often being referred to simply as: forming, storming, norming and performing.[16]

Forming

The team has been assembled and the task is allocated but team members don't know each other well enough to unconditionally trust each other. Spend time planning the task and getting to know each other as this will set an excellent foundation for the more challenging stage of storming.

Storming

The team has started to focus on delivering against the task, generating different ideas and solutions. At this stage it's entirely natural for differences of opinion and conflict to arise. If the team is prepared for this and it's managed well then this is a powerful and bonding stage as the team resolves its differences and moves towards consensus. On the other hand, if conflict is allowed to become personal, get out of hand and/or is not resolved constructively, the team may never trust one another and may become dysfunctional.

Norming

Assuming a positive outcome to the previous stage, then the team starts to move towards established processes and harmonious working practices. Each team member feels confident to take on their own role and deliver their part. As they become more established, build trust and continue to improve, the team reaches the optimum stage of performing.

Performing

This is where results are delivered and team members rely on each other and value their contribution. Some teams never reach the level of performing, probably due to meeting challenges along the way. Again, awareness is the key to a smooth journey and transition from forming to performing.

Of course, team members leave and change projects are completed, so Tuckman added on additional phases known as adjourning and transforming to cover these stages. Others have also used the term 'reforming'.

Using and sharing our knowledge about the stages of team development and team roles can be a really effective way of setting your Change Team up for success.

So what? Over to you...

1. In which of Belbin's roles are you naturally strongest? And which are less natural for you?

2. Which roles are missing from your current 'change league', and how might you address that?

Build your change league

3. What stage is your change team at, forming, storming, norming or performing? What challenges and opportunities does that stage present?

Day 8

Planning large-scale change

As Change Agents we're sometimes brought in to manage or deliver a change that's been presented as a fait accompli, including expectations and desired time frames that may not always be realistic. This is really difficult and puts us in the position of playing catch up. Here are seven fact-finding questions that can help you gather the information needed to build a robust communication plan and manage the change.

What is the change?

How could you explain the change in one sentence? For example: 'We are moving from paper-based appraisal to an online performance and talent management system.'

Planning large-scale change

Why do we need the change?

What's the reason for the change? What's the evidence or business rationale behind it? What happens if no change occurs? Gather as many reasons for change as possible that will resonate with all levels of the organization.

Example 1

> We need to compete better in the marketplace so we must transform ourselves into a high-performing business with better alignment against objectives and better visibility of high and low performers.

Example 2

> We need to increase retention of staff. Our current appraisal system doesn't result in development or career opportunities so people are leaving. A new system would help us to develop and retain talent.

Example 3

> Our paper-based HR systems aren't compliant. An electronic system will help us capture and retain data securely as well as automatically alerting us to certification expiry dates, helping to protect us as a business.

It's important that we can make the link between the change requirements, overall strategy and the individual. A useful phrase is 'which means that'; for example, 'We have a high attrition rate, which means that we are losing talent faster than the competition, which means that we are less able to innovate and compete, which means that we could go out of business within six months if we don't change now.'

What does success look like?

Success needs to be specific and tangible with goals and milestones. Where possible attach metrics to these to make sure that they're measurable.

Let's continue with the example of moving from a paper-based appraisal to an online system. What indicators would provide evidence that change is happening over the short term? Examples might be: the average number of objectives people have put in the system, or the frequency of logging into the system over the first three months. We need to set short-term metrics and goals that we can track because these will provide evidence as to whether the wider behaviours of the organization are changing.

How does this fit with other ongoing programmes and projects?

Do you need lots of HR or IT resource to roll out your initiative or is there something else already scheduled that could distract or derail your programme at the last minute? Ask this question as early as possible.

What and who is in scope?

Back to our project, now we need to consider what exactly is involved and who it will affect. Avoid 'scope creep', where the project becomes too large and uncontrollable and outgrows the original timescale and budget.

It's only during the scoping exercise that we sometimes start to realize some of the challenges that haven't been factored into the schedule. It's wise to break the changes down into small chunks, allowing us to complete and consolidate each activity before starting again.

In our earlier example, this might mean that we decide to focus on rolling out the core performance management functionality in year one and embed it within the whole business before moving on to incorporate talent management or 360-degree feedback. Or we might choose to roll full functionality out to a particular audience, perhaps as a pilot or a staggered roll-out. Either option has benefits and there are variations in between.

How will the change take place?

Here are four options for rolling out change.

The 'Big Bang' approach

Culture change can be easier to achieve using the 'Big Bang' approach – setting the milestones lower but involving a wider audience. In this way, we're more likely to get involvement from senior sponsors and there will be greater visibility. We can recognize quick wins and enforce consequences because we've been very clear about the overall behaviours and expectations.

Planning large-scale change

But it's important to be realistic about time frames and the complexity of the project. It's better to start simple and add functionality or complexity over time. It's also important to be realistic about how long any type of change is going to take. My recommendation would be to allow at least three years to achieve culture change.

Pilot

A pilot is a small-scale roll-out of a new process. But be careful. In some environments, simply using the term pilot may signal that it's an optional change that can be resisted or pushed back on, setting it up for failure.

Start by understanding what the purpose is of the pilot. How long will it run and what are the success measures and the audience? Who do you need to include to gain traction for the pilot?

Bear in mind that you and the provider will need to invest the same amount of time in setting up the system or project for a small short-term pilot as you would for a full-scale roll-out.

We're often requested to run a pilot in order to minimize risk, in which case one of the two following alternatives could be better options.

Proof of concept

There's likely to be an intent to work in partnership with external suppliers or an internal team. There may also be a nominal financial investment to indicate commitment but not yet contractual commitment to a large-scale roll-out. Once we have a proof of concept we can then involve a small group of people representative of the overall organization who can engage constructively with the system or service and provide feedback. The purpose is to provide tweaks and refinements that will improve the fit and support the roll-out. Those involved in the proof-of-concept evaluation may be ideal champions for the future roll-out and an indication of what the external company is like to work with.

Phased roll-out

This a pilot in disguise. Phased roll-out signals that this change is here to stay. It's just a matter of timing as to when it will affect everyone.

So, now let's consider the specific goals, outcomes and timelines.

Planning large-scale change

When is it happening?

Having scoped the project, audience and roll-out plan we can start to consider realistic time frames (although in the real world this often happens the other way around). Planning will shorten the implementation timelines as concerns and issues can be spotted in advance, messaging adjusted and diaries managed.

It's good to have a sense of urgency around a well-scoped and planned project, as people lose momentum when a change is too drawn-out – many changes are best managed in 6- to 12-week blocks.

So what? Over to you...

1. Which of the fact-finding questions do you need to focus on right now?

2. Try using 'which means that' to create some clearly articulated messages about the need for the change you're planning.

Planning large-scale change

3. Which of the options for rolling out change will work best for your project? Or do you need a combination?

Day 9

Build your communication plan

Well-planned proactive communication can overcome resistance and help individuals buy in to change before it's even necessary. Starting to plan three months ahead and rolling out the actual communications six weeks in advance is a good guideline.

When you're putting together a large-scale communication plan there are four stages to consider:

1. Understanding the audience.
2. Defining key messages.
3. Choosing a variety of methods to communicate.
4. Refining communications in line with feedback.

Build your communication plan

Understanding the audience

When considering your audience think about people's relationship to the change in terms of their role as well as their levels of impact, influence and power (and of course their personality). Using the term 'stakeholder' is a way of explaining the extent to which someone is affected by and/or can affect the change. Just a few key stakeholders can cause a project to succeed or fail.

During organizational change first consider the impact on employees. Then consider wider stakeholders such as customers, suppliers, trade unions or regulatory bodies. Some may be affected by the change and others may be able to impact the change; either way, they're still stakeholders.

Some initial questions to ask about stakeholders are as follows:

- Who will be directly/indirectly impacted by this change?
- How severe is the impact?
- Are they likely to perceive this as positive or negative change?
- How much power do they have as a group or individual?

- How much interest will they have in the change?

The four-box model below can help us categorize our stakeholders and help inform our communication plan.

Low power with high interest (vocalizers)	High power with high interest (key players)
Low power with low interest (peripherals)	High power with low interest (latents)

Key players

Stakeholders with high power and high interest can make or break a change so their early buy-in is important.

Latents

Keep stakeholders with high power and low interest informed as they can scupper a change at the last minute if kept out of the loop. By involving them in the early stages of change we can gain their commitment to support the project.

Vocalizers

Local Change Champions are useful in keeping stakeholders with low power and high interest frequently and positively informed.

Peripherals

Stakeholders with low power and low interest require less effort than the rest. They may just be informed of the change and any likely impact on them.

Obviously, these are broad and blunt classifications, so it's important as a change manager to keep an eye on each stakeholder's requirements as the change progresses because their power status may change.

Defining key messages

We need to consider which information is most relevant and/or motivational and therefore likely to encourage each set of stakeholders, whether internal or external, to buy in to the change. When we're building our communication plan, we need to be prepared to tailor our communications to cater to different perspectives.

What might be the likely objections to the change? Can these be pre-empted? Pre-empting objections is about answering the questions that are in people's heads before they ask them – it demonstrates that you understand their unspoken needs.

There's a helpful model that can be used to structure this type of communication effectively, known as 4MAT. It was originally developed by Bernice McCarthy (1980).[17] 4MAT asks four different questions when taking in information: why? what? how? and what if?

- 'Why' provides the reason and motivation to change.
- 'What' explains what the change is.
- 'How' questions are likely to be either practical or personal.
- 'What if' is about understanding the potential implications of us making the change or not.

Let's consider an example.

The change

A manufacturing business needs to move people from shift-based working with overtime to annualized hours, which means that the hours they're required to work will vary from week to week and overtime won't be payable.

Why?

- The parent company is demanding cost savings to deliver greater profitability.
- The marketplace has become extremely competitive and margins are being cut.
- Annualized hours are common practice for other competitors.

What?

- Staff will move from working fixed shifts to a variable working week that will be adjusted in line with demand.
- Overtime will no longer be available.
- The trade unions have been consulted and are reluctantly supportive.

How?

- This will be implemented from 1 April.
- Specific consultation on individual contracts will be available throughout February.

- Salaries will be averaged out over 12 months to allow for fluctuations.

What if we do?

- We will save enough money to remain open in the UK.
- A proportion of this revenue will be reinvested into R&D on this site.
- We will be able to keep 100% of current manufacturing jobs.

What if we don't?

- The factory will continue to be loss-making.
- 30% of jobs will need to be cut within 18 months.
- A proportion of the factory will be relocated to China.

I've given three bullets in each area for ease, but don't let this restrict you. Use this as the basis for all communications to make corporate change communication influential and compelling for the maximum number of people.

Build your communication plan

Choosing a variety of methods to communicate

It's not surprising that change doesn't happen when simply sent out in an uninspiring email. Other potentially more engaging options include:

- Posters, websites or webpages/intranet pages with FAQs.
- Involve marketing and develop a brand for our change along with themed items.
- Face-to-face communication.
- Inspirational PowerPoint presentations or videos.
- Asking key sponsors to create individual video clips.
- Video clips of people adopting the change or sharing their views about it.
- Asking managers to discuss to share information at team meetings.
- Audio files or podcasts for employees who travel a lot.
- Social media to reinforce key messages.

As the Change Agent, you may be planning the communications but not necessarily delivering them, so you need to find ways of ensuring that the communications are well shared by others. Provide your Change League with key message 'crib sheets' and give them the opportunity to practise and rehearse the change story so they can deliver it with authenticity.

Plan regular communication updates at every available opportunity. Communicate the progress and the 'quick wins' widely and deal with those who are not progressing with a quiet word. Update the senior board with monthly or quarterly information – make it visual and consider the use of statistics of take-up or league tables.

If we put thought and effort into the types of communications that we deliver and make them relevant and influential, then they're far more likely to have the desired impact.

Refining communications in line with feedback

Be prepared to seek feedback along the way, and to understand how the messaging is being received. Are there certain questions that are being asked that we haven't prepared answers for? Perhaps we can update our FAQs or Change Agent crib sheets to accommodate these, or release a video responding to some of them. Or we could survey certain stakeholders.

If our messaging it being misinterpreted, adapt or clarify it. It helps to communicate clearly, consistently

Build your communication plan

and with empathy. We need to look for positives and early signs of success and be sure to share these with others to reinforce the behaviours of those who are changing.

✎ So what? Over to you...

1. Who are your key stakeholders, and how can you ensure their buy-in as early as possible?

2. Try crafting a 4MAT message for a particularly tricky stakeholder.

Build your communication plan

3. What other types of communication could you add into the mix along with emails to reach and engage people more effectively?

Day 10
The process of large-scale change

Psychologist Kurt Lewin (1951) saw change as a three-step approach, a process rather than an event.[18] In order to make a change, he said, we have to:

1. 'Unfreeze' the status quo
2. Make the actual 'change'
3. Reset or 'refreeze' the new way of doing things.

If we don't complete this final refreezing stage, we'll almost certainly swing back to the old status quo.

The process of large-scale change

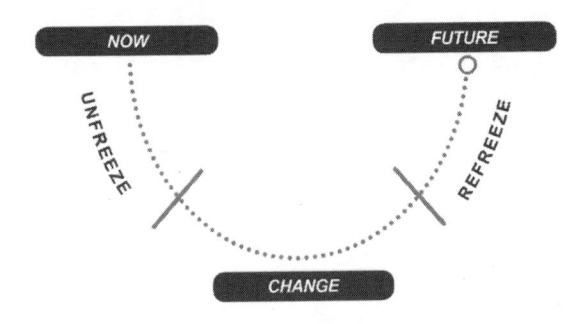

Fig. 6 Lewin's change theory

Explaining why change fails

It's often at a transition stage in this three-step model that change becomes derailed, usually through people issues. Commonly raised issues include lack of:

- buy-in/resistance to change
- sponsorship/role-modelling
- communication
- sense of urgency
- clear vision
- impetus/follow-through
- resources.

So what can Change Agents do about these blockers to change? Change only happens if there are more driving forces than resisting ones. This may require creating additional driving forces such as communicating the change better or creating a clearer vision of the future, or removing the key resistors; for example, persuading people of the benefits of the change so that they become drivers rather than resistors.

Kotter's eight-step process for change

John Kotter also sees change as a process with several defined stages. His eight-step process spells out the practical steps of making organizational change stick, and it's invaluable for both planning change and diagnosing why and where change has failed.

Establish a sense of urgency

The term 'burning platform' is sometimes used to create an urgent reason for change. This powerful but unpleasant metaphor apparently stems from the Piper Alpha oil rig fire in 1988. If the oil rig platform you're standing on is on fire, the decision is made for you; your life's at stake so, of course, you jump. Clearly, we don't want to push people into life-or-death situations in order to make change happen.

The process of large-scale change

However, it's a powerful concept – establishing urgency around moving away from danger (the fire) and/or towards a positive future of safety (the lifeboat) will help change happen faster.

Think about both the 'towards motivators' (i.e. a positive future) and the 'dangers' of staying the same, in order to create a sense of urgency.

Form a powerful guiding coalition

This is likely to be your Change Team: a group of people working together to see the change through. At the 'unfreezing' stage, include senior sponsors as well as other Change Agents or 'doers'. You might start with a smaller steering group to define, plan and lead the change, and then expand this by engaging other champions or Change Teams who may be closer to the intended change and can ensure that any suggested plans are achievable.

System change can be fraught with issues if those who proposed it aren't connected with the realities of implementing it within a specific time frame. It's a good idea to bring people in at the planning stage who have relevant specialist knowledge, even if they must be trusted to maintain confidentiality.

Create a compelling vision

The Change Team needs to consider what the 'change story' is. It's likely to have elements of the burning platform concept outlined earlier but it generally needs to be positive, to motivate people towards a better future. Shareholders may be motivated by share price but for employees, job security or opportunities for development are likely to be more compelling as a future vision.

Communicate the change

Change starts to become real as we communicate in order to initiate it on a wider scale. This is one of the first places that change frequently fails. Reasons for failure include poor preparation during steps one to three, or people falling into the trap of considering change to be an event rather than a process.

Communication is a two-way process so it's not enough to simply dictate change or expect it to happen as a result of a series of emails. Communicating change includes listening and responding to people's concerns, helping them to buy in and dealing with any associated emotions around the change. As outlined in the previous chapter, use a variety of media to increase the chances of being heard by everyone.

The process of large-scale change

Remove obstacles

With the right skills, your guiding coalition will already have already identified blockers that need addressing. This stage is all about getting rid of the obstacles that are pushing against the new way such as systems, structures or attitudes and behaviours.

Create short-term wins

We're now moving back up Lewin's Change Curve into the refreeze section, and into another key transition where change can succeed or fail. Noticing and celebrating short-term wins allows us to promote the success of the change programme in three ways:

1. It motivates and recognizes those early adopters.
2. It clearly signals to those in denial that the change is real, and that it's here to stay.
3. It demonstrates some of the benefits of the change and makes the new way of doing things habitual.

This is a time for publicly recognizing those who have got on board with the change and privately nudging those who haven't.

Getting the right personalities in place at each stage of change maximizes our chances of driving things through into a 'refreeze' and ensuring value is derived from our change.

Consolidate improvements

Many organizations who go through mergers are held back by legacy systems. Having people still on old terms and conditions makes it difficult to embed a new recruitment policy, for example.

It's important that the Change Team has the focus and enthusiasm to drive things through to completion at this stage.

Institutionalize the change

The final step, in Kotter's terms, is 'institutionalizing the new approach'; that is, embedding the change. It's essentially building on step seven and taking it to completion.

Overlaying Lewin's unfreeze-change-refreeze model on to Kotter's eight steps helps us to better understand the danger points where change breaks down. If we follow Kotter's eight-step process consistently and enlist the different skills of our

The process of large-scale change

Change League as required, it's easy to see how we could gain greater, faster value from change in our organizations.

> ### ✏️ So what? Over to you...
>
> 1. Think about a change in your organization. What are the drivers and resistors? This will help you come up with a strategy of who and what needs to be addressed if the change is to be successful.

2. How many of Kotter's eight stages do you recognize in your organization? Where are you right now?

The process of large-scale change

3. Thinking ahead, how can you ensure you embed the change you're seeking in your organization?

Conclusion

Anyone can be an effective Change Agent if they are open-minded and committed to putting these 10 lessons into practice. Those who can adapt to change and help others to do the same can soften the human impact of change considerably, and also increase the chances of the change delivering the intended results. It all starts with having the courage to stand up and be counted, together with insight into the way others are motivated and how they process information.

We can start small by understanding ourselves and then branch out, considering the preferences of our colleagues and the composition of our teams.

A good way to begin is by reflecting on changes that you've experienced and evaluating what worked and what could have been improved. If you'd been directly involved, what could you have done that would have made a difference?

People find it reassuring to understand that the emotions they're feeling while going through change are completely normal and part of a natural process. Sharing models of team roles or personality

Conclusion

preferences is a great way to engage with colleagues about individual differences and the impact this may have on the way we process change.

You have everything you need to be an amazing Change Agent – now go Do Change Better!

Endnotes

[1] J. M. Burns, *Transforming Leadership* (New York: Grove Press, 2003).

[2] B. M. Bass, *Transformational Leadership* (London: Psychology Press, 2005).

[3] D. Sivers, *How to start a movement*. TED Talk, 2010. Retrieved from www.ted.com/talks/derek_sivers_how_to_start_a_movement

[4] R. Beckhard and R. T. Harris, *Organizational Transitions: Managing complex change* (Addison-Wesley, 1987).

[5] L. Porter and S. J. Tanner, *Assessing Business Excellence* (2nd edn) (Oxford: Routledge, 2003).

[6] E. Locke and G. Latham, 'Goal-Setting Theory', in J. B. Miner (ed.), *Organizational Behaviour 1*, (New York: Routledge, 1994), pp. 159–183.

[7] K. W. Chan and R. Mauborgne, 'Tipping point leadership', *Harvard Business Review* (April 2003), 79–98.

[8] R. B. Cialdini, *Influence: The psychology of persuasion* (2006).

[9] A. Meharabian, *Silent Messages: Implicit communication of emotions and attitudes* (2nd edn) (Belmont, CA: Wadsworth, 1981).

Endnotes

[10] S. Covey, *The 7 Habits of Highly Effective People* (New York: Simon and Schuster, 1989).

[11] E. Kübler-Ross, *On Death and Dying* (Vol. 22) (New York: Macmillan, 1969).

[12] E. H. Schein, 'Coming to a new awareness of organizational culture', *Sloan Management Review*, 25(2), 3 (1984).

[13] R. Quinn and K. S. Cameron, *Diagnosing and Changing Organizational Culture: Based on the Competing Values Framework* (New York: John Wiley & Sons, 2006).

[14] G. Johnson, K. Scholes and R. Whittington, *Exploring Corporate Strategy* (Harlow: Prentice Hall, 1999).

[15] M. Belbin, *Management Teams* (3rd edn) (Abingdon: Routledge, 2010). Retrieved from www.belbin.com

[16] B. Tuckman, 'Developmental sequence in small groups', *Psychological Bulletin*, 63(6), 384–399 (1965).

[17] B. McCarthy, *The 4MAT System* (Boston: About Learning, 1980).

[18] K. Lewin, *Field Theories in Social Science* (New York: Harper & Brothers, 1951).

Enjoyed this?
Then you'll love...

How to be a Change Superhero: The business toolkit to help you to 'do' change better by Lucinda Carney

Most of us have experienced change being 'done' to us – badly. It really doesn't have to be that way!

This book is for managers who have tried to deliver business change but felt frustrated and disempowered by the experience. It's for people who want to stand up and make a difference, igniting and inspiring successful change, but don't know where to start. This book is a complete toolkit for aspiring Change Superheroes!

Lucinda Carney C.Psychol uses her decades of business experience to:

- Explain the repeated, human causes of failed change.
- Uncover the secrets to delivering sustainable change.

Enjoyed this? Then you'll love...

- Provide prospective Change Superheroes with the confidence to deliver their own successful business change.
- Share case studies, downloadable tools and real-life examples of successful change.

Let's change the way we do Change!

Lucinda Carney is a Chartered Occupational Psychologist with many years' corporate HR experience leading and delivering system and culture change. In her role as CEO and founder of Actus Software she works with a wide variety of business professionals in a range of sectors and shares that knowledge through powerful case studies.

Lucinda hosts the fast-growing and number-one-ranking *HR Uprising* podcast. She won the Everywoman Entrepreneur of the Year Award in 2016. A member of the BPS, CIPD and the Centre for Evidence Based Management (CEBma), she lives in Hertfordshire with her husband and two children and is a keen netball player in her spare time.

Other 6-Minute Smarts titles

Write to Think (based on *Exploratory Writing* by Alison Jones)

No-Nonsense PR (based on Hype Yourself by Lucy Werner)

How to be Happy at Work (based on *My Job Isn't Working!* by Michael Brown)

Mastering People Management (based on *Mission: To Manage* by Marianne Page)

Present Like a Pro (based on *Executive Presentations* by Jacqui Harper)

Look out for more titles coming soon! Visit www.practicalinspiration.com for all our latest titles.